MAD LIBS®

CAMP DAZE MAD LIBS

By Roger Price and Leonard Stern

Mad Libs
An Imprint of Penguin Random House

MAD LIBS
Penguin Young Readers Group
An Imprint of Penguin Random House LLC

Concept created by Roger Price & Leonard Stern

Published by Mad Libs,
an imprint of Penguin Random House LLC,
345 Hudson Street, New York, New York 10014.
Printed in the USA.

ISBN 9780843122398

43 45 47 49 50 48 46 44

MAD LIBS® is a game for people who don't like games!
It can be played by one, two, three, four, or forty.

• RIDICULOUSLY SIMPLE DIRECTIONS

In this tablet you will find stories containing blank spaces where words are left out. One player, the READER, selects one of these stories. The READER does not tell anyone what the story is about. Instead, he/she asks the other players, the WRITERS, to give him/her words. These words are used to fill in the blank spaces in the story.

• TO PLAY

The READER asks each WRITER in turn to call out a word—an adjective or a noun or whatever the space calls for—and uses them to fill in the blank spaces in the story. The result is a MAD LIBS® game.

When the READER then reads the completed MAD LIBS® game to the other players, they will discover that they have written a story that is fantastic, screamingly funny, shocking, silly, crazy, or just plain dumb—depending upon which words each WRITER called out.

• EXAMPLE (*Before* and *After*)

"_____ !" he said _____
            EXCLAMATION   ADVERB

as he jumped into his convertible _____ and
                                              NOUN

drove off with his _____ wife.
                              ADJECTIVE

"_____*Ouch!*_____ !" he said _____*stupidly*_____
            EXCLAMATION   ADVERB

as he jumped into his convertible _____*cat*_____ and
                                              NOUN

drove off with his _____*brave*_____ wife.
                              ADJECTIVE

MAD LIBS®
QUICK REVIEW

In case you have forgotten what adjectives, adverbs, nouns, and verbs are, here is a quick review:

An ADJECTIVE describes something or somebody. *Lumpy, soft, ugly, messy,* and *short* are adjectives.

An ADVERB tells how something is done. It modifies a verb and usually ends in "ly." *Modestly, stupidly, greedily,* and *carefully* are adverbs.

A NOUN is the name of a person, place or thing. *Sidewalk, umbrella, bridle, bathtub,* and *nose* are nouns.

A VERB is an action word. *Run, pitch, jump,* and *swim* are verbs. Put the verbs in past tense if the directions say PAST TENSE. *Ran, pitched, jumped,* and *swam* are verbs in the past tense.

When we ask for a PLACE, we mean any sort of place: a country or city *(Spain, Cleveland)* or a room *(bathroom, kitchen.)*

An EXCLAMATION or SILLY WORD is any sort of funny sound, gasp, grunt, or outcry, like *Wow!, Ouch!, Whomp!, Ick!,* and *Gadzooks!*

When we ask for specific words, like a NUMBER, a COLOR, an ANIMAL, or a PART OF THE BODY, we mean a word that is one of those things, like *seven, blue, horse,* or *head.*

When we ask for a PLURAL, it means more than one. For example, *cat* pluralized is *cats.*

MAD LIBS® is fun to play with friends, but you can also play it by yourself! To begin with, DO NOT look at the story on the page below. Fill in the blanks on this page with the words called for. Then, using the words you have selected, fill in the blank spaces in the story.

Now you've created your own hilarious MAD LIBS® game!

INTRODUCTION

ADJECTIVE _____

ADJECTIVE _____

NOUN _____

VERB ENDING IN "ING" _____

PLURAL NOUN _____

PART OF THE BODY (PLURAL) _____

VERB ENDING IN "ING" _____

NOUN _____

TYPE OF INEXPENSIVE FOOD_____

PLURAL NOUN _____

PLURAL NOUN _____

NUMBER _____

NOUN _____

PART OF THE BODY _____

NOUN _____

ADVERB_____

NOUN _____

Once again, it is the time of year when parents can get rid of their

_____ kids by sending them to a/an _____
ADJECTIVE   ADJECTIVE

summer camp. Today they are mostly "theme camps." There are foot-

ball camps, computer camps, _____ camps, _____
                              NOUN   VERB ENDING IN "ING"

camps, and special camps for children who like to make ceramic

_____ with their _____. These camps
PLURAL NOUN   PART OF THE BODY (PLURAL)

have classes in _____ and in remedial _____.
                VERB ENDING IN "ING"   NOUN

But all summer, camps feed the kids _____ and
                                      TYPE OF INEXPENSIVE FOOD

make them sleep in _____ or rickety _____. Every
                    PLURAL NOUN   PLURAL NOUN

kid has a counselor who is a big _____-year-old _____
                                  NUMBER   NOUN

who doesn't know his _____ from his _____.
                      PART OF THE BODY   NOUN

But kids _____ put up with these indignities because
          ADVERB

they love camp and hate to go back to their own _____.
                                                  NOUN

MAD LIBS® is fun to play with friends, but you can also play it by yourself! To begin with, DO NOT look at the story on the page below. Fill in the blanks on this page with the words called for. Then, using the words you have selected, fill in the blank spaces in the story.

Now you've created your own hilarious MAD LIBS® game!

TENNIS

ADJECTIVE_____

PLURAL NOUN _____

ADJECTIVE_____

ADJECTIVE_____

PLURAL NOUN _____

NOUN _____

ADJECTIVE_____

NOUN _____

NOUN _____

VERB _____

NOUN _____

ADJECTIVE_____

PART OF THE BODY _____

ADVERB_____

NOUN _____

NOUN _____

EXCLAMATION_____

MAD LIBS®
TENNIS

The most important game you will play at camp is tennis. Tennis is

popular with young people, _____ people, and even
                              ADJECTIVE

with elderly _____ . Playing tennis gets you out in the
             PLURAL NOUN

_____ air and is really _____ exercise. You
   ADJECTIVE   ADJECTIVE

can wear special _____ made especially for the court.
                    PLURAL NOUN

The most important part of tennis is the serve. To serve, you throw

the _____ high in the air and hit it into your opponent's
      NOUN

_____ _____ . Then you rush up to the
   ADJECTIVE   NOUN

_____ and _____ . The various strokes in
    NOUN   VERB

tennis are called the "overhand _____," the "_____
                                   NOUN   ADJECTIVE

volley," and the "back-_____ return." And, if you win, you
                      PART OF THE BODY

must remember to run up and leap _____ over the
                                      ADVERB

_____ . Then slap your opponent on the _____
   NOUN   NOUN

and say, "_____ !"
            EXCLAMATION

MAD LIBS® is fun to play with friends, but you can also play it by yourself! To begin with, DO NOT look at the story on the page below. Fill in the blanks on this page with the words called for. Then, using the words you have selected, fill in the blank spaces in the story.

Now you've created your own hilarious MAD LIBS® game!

KITCHEN INSPECTION

PLURAL NOUN _____

ADJECTIVE _____

ADJECTIVE _____

PART OF THE BODY (PLURAL) _____

ADJECTIVE _____

ANIMAL (PLURAL) _____

ANIMAL (PLURAL) _____

PLURAL NOUN _____

CELEBRITY _____

NOUN _____

TYPE OF BIRD _____

NOUN _____

NOUN _____

TYPE OF LIQUID _____

PLURAL NOUN _____

NOUN _____

SOMETHING GREASY _____

SOMETHING HEALTHY _____

ADJECTIVE _____

MAD LIBS®
KITCHEN INSPECTION

Inspectors from the State Department of Health and _____
_____ PLURAL NOUN

came here today to inspect the _____ kitchen and to
_____ ADJECTIVE

make sure that our _____ cooks were washing their
_____ ADJECTIVE

_____ before preparing our _____ meals.
PART OF THE BODY (PLURAL) _____ ADJECTIVE

And that there are no little _____ or _____
_____ ANIMAL (PLURAL) _____ ANIMAL (PLURAL)

running around in the kitchen and spreading _____.
_____ PLURAL NOUN

They checked the lunch prepared by our dietician, _____.
_____ CELEBRITY

We had spaghetti and _____ balls. On Tuesdays, we have
_____ NOUN

boiled _____ with rice. On Wednesdays, we have a choice
_____ TYPE OF BIRD

of _____ soup or a/an _____ omelette with
_____ NOUN _____ NOUN

_____ sauce. The inspector found a lot of _____
TYPE OF LIQUID _____ PLURAL NOUN

in the salad and said there was too much _____ in the
_____ NOUN

milk. In the future, we will have less _____ to eat and
_____ SOMETHING GREASY

more _____. But I bet it will still taste _____.
_____ SOMETHING HEALTHY _____ ADJECTIVE

MAD LIBS® is fun to play with friends, but you can also play it by yourself! To begin with, DO NOT look at the story on the page below. Fill in the blanks on this page with the words called for. Then, using the words you have selected, fill in the blank spaces in the story.

Now you've created your own hilarious MAD LIBS® game!

OUR FAVORITE COUNSELOR

ADJECTIVE _____

PERSON IN ROOM (MALE) _____

PERSON IN ROOM (FEMALE) _____

NOUN _____

NOUN _____

ADJECTIVE _____

PLURAL NOUN _____

NOUN _____

PLURAL NOUN _____

SAME PERSON IN ROOM (MALE) _____

ADJECTIVE _____

COUNTRY _____

PLURAL NOUN _____

PART OF THE BODY _____

PLURAL NOUN _____

PLURAL NOUN _____

NOUN _____

ADJECTIVE _____

MAD LIBS®
OUR FAVORITE COUNSELOR

It is very difficult to choose our most _____ counselor.
ADJECTIVE

_____ and _____ are running neck
PERSON IN ROOM (MALE) PERSON IN ROOM (FEMALE)

and _____ in this hotly contested _____.
NOUN NOUN

Both counselors can be described as _____ natured
ADJECTIVE

_____ who are seldom without a/an _____
PLURAL NOUN NOUN

on their _____. _____ is in charge of
PLURAL NOUN SAME PERSON IN ROOM (MALE)

the waterfront and is a/an _____ lifeguard, certified by the
ADJECTIVE

_____ Red Cross to teach swimming, paddling of our
COUNTRY

_____, and to give mouth-to-_____
PLURAL NOUN PART OF THE BODY

resuscitation. He is a former actor who appeared in many Broadway

_____. He was also on the television soap opera "All
PLURAL NOUN

My _____." We are sure that no matter who is
PLURAL NOUN

chosen as our favorite _____, the other will be a very
NOUN

_____ sport about our decision.
ADJECTIVE

MAD LIBS® is fun to play with friends, but you can also play it by yourself! To begin with, DO NOT look at the story on the page below. Fill in the blanks on this page with the words called for. Then, using the words you have selected, fill in the blank spaces in the story.

Now you've created your own hilarious MAD LIBS® game!

BASKETBALL

CAMP NAME _____

ANIMAL (PLURAL) _____

ANOTHER CAMP NAME _____

ANIMAL (PLURAL) _____

NUMBER _____

CELEBRITY _____

NOUN _____

CELEBRITY (MALE) _____

NOUN _____

PERSON IN ROOM _____

NOUN _____

NOUN _____

PLURAL NOUN _____

NUMBER _____

ADJECTIVE _____

PERSON IN ROOM (MALE) _____

CELEBRITY _____

PERSON IN ROOM (FEMALE) _____

MAD LIBS®
BASKETBALL

"Ladies and gentlemen, here we are at the championship basketball

game between the _____ _____ and the
                   CAMP NAME   ANIMAL (PLURAL)

_____ _____ . The _____-foot center
ANOTHER CAMP NAME   ANIMAL (PLURAL)   NUMBER

has just tipped the ball to _____ , who dribbles down
                                CELEBRITY

the _____ and passes to _____ . Oh, too
        NOUN   CELEBRITY (MALE)

bad! He just committed a/an _____ . That means
                                    NOUN

_____ gets two free throws. He/She drops the
PERSON IN ROOM

_____ right in the _____ . And the second as well. This
    NOUN   NOUN

means two _____ and makes the score _____ to nothing.
            PLURAL NOUN   NUMBER

Wow! What a/an _____ game. If our team loses, our
                    ADJECTIVE

coach, _____ will be replaced by _____ .
        PERSON IN ROOM (MALE)   CELEBRITY

Or maybe even _____ ."
                PERSON IN ROOM (FEMALE)

From CAMP DAZE MAD LIBS® • Copyright © 2001, 1988 by Penguin Random House LLC.

MAD LIBS® is fun to play with friends, but you can also play it by yourself! To begin with, DO NOT look at the story on the page below. Fill in the blanks on this page with the words called for. Then, using the words you have selected, fill in the blank spaces in the story.

Now you've created your own hilarious MAD LIBS® game!

SAFETY PRECAUTIONS FOR CAMPERS

NOUN _____

ADJECTIVE _____

ADJECTIVE _____

SILLY WORD _____

NOUN _____

SOMETHING ALIVE _____

TYPE OF LIQUID _____

ANIMAL _____

EXCLAMATION _____

NUMBER _____

PLURAL NOUN _____

NOUN _____

PLACE _____

TYPE OF FOOD (PLURAL) _____

NOUN _____

ADVERB _____

MAD LIBS®
SAFETY PRECAUTIONS
FOR CAMPERS

Attention all campers! Just a few weeks ago you were a miserable

_____ , living in the _____ city with your
NOUN   ADJECTIVE

_____ parents. But a few weeks at Camp _____
ADJECTIVE   SILLY WORD

will turn you into a self-reliant, fearless _____ . But, you
NOUN

must learn to exist in the wild.

Rule One: If you catch a/an _____ and make a fire to cook
                              SOMETHING ALIVE

it, always remember to pour _____ on the fire when you're
                              TYPE OF LIQUID

through. Smokey the _____ always says, "_____!"
                      ANIMAL   EXCLAMATION

Rule Two: Do not go more than _____ yards away from the trail.
                                NUMBER

If you get lost, remember that _____ always grow on the
                                PLURAL NOUN

north side of a/an _____ . If you have a compass, the
                    NOUN

needle will always point toward _____ . If you run into a
                                  PLACE

bear, do not give it _____ . Just be calm and climb a/an
                      TYPE OF FOOD (PLURAL)

_____ .
NOUN

If you follow these rules, you can live very _____ in the woods.
                                              ADVERB

MAD LIBS® is fun to play with friends, but you can also play it by yourself! To begin with, DO NOT look at the story on the page below. Fill in the blanks on this page with the words called for. Then, using the words you have selected, fill in the blank spaces in the story.

Now you've created your own hilarious MAD LIBS® game!

CHESS

VERB _____

CELEBRITY _____

SILLY WORD_____

PLURAL NOUN _____

ADJECTIVE_____

ADJECTIVE_____

NOUN _____

PLURAL NOUN _____

NOUN _____

PROFESSION _____

NOUN _____

EXCLAMATION_____

EXCLAMATION_____

PART OF THE BODY _____

PERSON IN ROOM _____

NUMBER _____

ADJECTIVE_____

NATIONALITY _____

MAD LIBS®
CHESS

Some camps love to _____ chess. Chess is an ancient
                        VERB

game invented by _____. A similar game called
                        CELEBRITY

_____ was played by Chinese _____
SILLY WORD   PLURAL NOUN

in the fourth century. It requires _____ concentration
                                        ADJECTIVE

and a/an _____ mind. It is played on a square _____
            ADJECTIVE   NOUN

by moving thirty-two little _____. The pieces are called
                                PLURAL NOUN

"the King" and "the Queen" and "the _____," and the
                                            NOUN

"_____." The object is to capture your opponent's
    PROFESSION

_____. When you threaten his king, you must say,
    NOUN

"_____!" and if you win, you say, "_____!"
    EXCLAMATION   EXCLAMATION

A chess player must sit in one place for hours at a time. This is very

hard on his _____. Sometimes a famous champion
                PART OF THE BODY

like _____ will play _____ different people all at
        PERSON IN ROOM   NUMBER

once. Most champion chess players are very _____.
                                                    ADJECTIVE

Many of them are also _____.
                            NATIONALITY

MAD LIBS® is fun to play with friends, but you can also play it by yourself! To begin with, DO NOT look at the story on the page below. Fill in the blanks on this page with the words called for. Then, using the words you have selected, fill in the blank spaces in the story.

Now you've created your own hilarious MAD LIBS® game!

LONG DISTANCE RUNNING

ADJECTIVE _____

SILLY FIRST NAME _____

ADJECTIVE _____

VERB ENDING IN "ING" _____

VERB ENDING IN "ING" _____

TYPE OF FOOD _____

COLOR _____

PLURAL NOUN _____

NUMBER _____

PART OF THE BODY (PLURAL) _____

PART OF THE BODY (PLURAL) _____

VERB ENDING IN "ING" _____

NUMBER _____

NUMBER _____

PLURAL NOUN _____

CITY _____

ADJECTIVE _____

NOUN _____

MAD☺LIBS®
LONG DISTANCE RUNNING

For years, everyone thought the four-minute mile was a/an _____
                                                          ADJECTIVE

dream. Now every camper named Tom, Dick, and _____
                                                SILLY FIRST NAME

can do it because of new _____ training methods.
                          ADJECTIVE

Distance runners have to give up _____ and
                                  VERB ENDING IN "ING"

_____. They eat lots of _____ and plenty
VERB ENDING IN "ING"   TYPE OF FOOD

of fresh _____ vegetables and lots of _____.
          COLOR   PLURAL NOUN

Every morning they spend _____ hours stretching their
                          NUMBER

_____ and touching their _____.
PART OF THE BODY (PLURAL)   PART OF THE BODY (PLURAL)

Then they spend two hours _____ until their pulse gets
                           VERB ENDING IN "ING"

up to _____. Then they do _____ laps around the track. All
       NUMBER   NUMBER

of this strengthens their _____ so they will be ready to run
                           PLURAL NOUN

the _____ Marathon. You can always tell a serious runner
     CITY

by the _____ expression on his _____.
        ADJECTIVE   NOUN

From CAMP DAZE MAD LIBS® • Copyright © 2001, 1988 by Penguin Random House LLC.

MAD LIBS® is fun to play with friends, but you can also play it by yourself! To begin with, DO NOT look at the story on the page below. Fill in the blanks on this page with the words called for. Then, using the words you have selected, fill in the blank spaces in the story.

Now you've created your own hilarious MAD LIBS® game!

TELEVISION LISTINGS

NOUN _____

NOUN _____

PLURAL NOUN _____

ADJECTIVE _____

PERSON IN ROOM _____

NOUN _____

CELEBRITY _____

PLURAL NOUN _____

VERB ENDING IN "ING" _____

PERSON IN ROOM (LAST NAME) _____

TYPE OF SPORT _____

NOUN _____

PLACE _____

ADJECTIVE _____

NOUN _____

PERSON IN ROOM (MALE) _____

CELEBRITY _____

NOUN _____

CITY _____

ADJECTIVE _____

PLURAL NOUN _____

PLURAL NOUN _____

ADVERB _____

MAD LIBS®
TELEVISION LISTINGS

For those campers who have a cold or poison _____ and
NOUN

are forced to stay in their _____ for the day, here is a list
NOUN

of television _____ you can watch.
PLURAL NOUN

7:00 A.M. The _____ Early News. With _____
ADJECTIVE _PERSON IN ROOM_

as the anchor _____ and _____
NOUN _CELEBRITY_

giving the weather. Special report on retirement homes

for old _____ and teenage _____.
PLURAL NOUN _VERB ENDING IN "ING"_

10:00 A.M. The _____ $50,000 Invitational
PERSON IN ROOM (LAST NAME)

Pro-Am _____ Tournament. Held at the
TYPE OF SPORT

famous _____ Club in _____.
NOUN _PLACE_

11:00 A.M. The _____ movie today is "Rambo Breaks His
ADJECTIVE

_____," and it stars _____ as
NOUN _PERSON IN ROOM (MALE)_

Rambo's father and _____ as his _____.
CELEBRITY _NOUN_

In this picture, Rambo kills everyone in _____.
CITY

2:00 P.M. Documentary about _____ animals living on the
ADJECTIVE

African _____. A study of lions, tigers, and
PLURAL NOUN

_____. Should be viewed _____.
PLURAL NOUN _ADVERB_

From CAMP DAZE MAD LIBS® • Copyright © 2001, 1988 by Penguin Random House LLC.

MAD LIBS® is fun to play with friends, but you can also play it by yourself! To begin with, DO NOT look at the story on the page below. Fill in the blanks on this page with the words called for. Then, using the words you have selected, fill in the blank spaces in the story.

Now you've created your own hilarious MAD LIBS® game!

THE CONSTITUTION

ADJECTIVE _____

PLURAL NOUN _____

ADJECTIVE _____

PLURAL NOUN _____

ADJECTIVE _____

PLURAL NOUN _____

PLURAL NOUN _____

PLURAL NOUN _____

PLURAL NOUN _____

ADJECTIVE _____

PLURAL NOUN _____

ADJECTIVE _____

PLURAL NOUN _____

MAD LIBS®
THE CONSTITUTION

Studying the Constitution is a/an _____ rainy day camp
                                        ADJECTIVE

activity. In 1787, a convention of important American _____
                                                         PLURAL NOUN

ratified our constitution. The Constitution was a/an _____
                                                          ADJECTIVE

document which guaranteed that the U.S. would not merely be a

league of independent _____, but a nation with a/an
                          PLURAL NOUN

_____ government that would deal with _____
   ADJECTIVE   PLURAL NOUN

as well as _____. The Constitution provided for a
               PLURAL NOUN

senate, to which every state would send two _____, and
                                                 PLURAL NOUN

a larger body called the House of _____, which was based
                                       PLURAL NOUN

on population. The government was divided into three branches:

the judicial, the legislative, and the _____. This created
                                            ADJECTIVE

a system of checks and _____ that works to protect us to
                           PLURAL NOUN

this day and gives us our _____ government of the
                              ADJECTIVE

people, for the people, and by the _____.
                                       PLURAL NOUN

MAD LIBS® is fun to play with friends, but you can also play it by yourself! To begin with, DO NOT look at the story on the page below. Fill in the blanks on this page with the words called for. Then, using the words you have selected, fill in the blank spaces in the story.

Now you've created your own hilarious MAD LIBS® game!

CAMPFIRE STORIES

PLURAL NOUN _____

ADJECTIVE _____

PLURAL NOUN _____

ADJECTIVE _____

ADJECTIVE _____

NOUN _____

PERSON IN ROOM (LAST NAME) _____

LAST NAME OF PERSON _____

PLACE _____

ANOTHER LAST NAME _____

PART OF THE BODY _____

TYPE OF LIQUID _____

ARTICLE OF CLOTHING (PLURAL) _____

RELATIVE _____

PIECE OF FURNITURE _____

VERB ENDING IN "ING" _____

ADJECTIVE _____

MAD☺LIBS®
CAMPFIRE STORIES

It is always fun to chop up some _____ and use them to
PLURAL NOUN

build a/an _____ campfire. Then you get all of the
ADJECTIVE

_____ to sit around the fire and tell scary stories. You can
PLURAL NOUN

tell about Ichabod Crane, the _____ schoolteacher of Sleepy
ADJECTIVE

Hollow and his _____ adventures with the headless _____.
ADJECTIVE   NOUN

Or you can tell "The Fall of the House of _____,"
PERSON IN ROOM (LAST NAME)

which was written by Edgar Allen _____. Or you
LAST NAME OF PERSON

can tell about vampires from _____, like the terrible Count
PLACE

_____, who bit people on the _____
ANOTHER LAST NAME OF PERSON   PART OF THE BODY

and drank their _____. By this time, many of the young
TYPE OF LIQUID

campers will start shaking in their _____ and
ARTICLE OF CLOTHING (PLURAL)

will begin yelling for their _____ and go hide under the
RELATIVE

_____. Believe me, when it comes to _____
PIECE OF FURNITURE   VERB ENDING IN "ING"

a bunch of kids, there's nothing like a real _____ ghost story.
ADJECTIVE

MAD LIBS® is fun to play with friends, but you can also play it by yourself! To begin with, DO NOT look at the story on the page below. Fill in the blanks on this page with the words called for. Then, using the words you have selected, fill in the blank spaces in the story.

Now you've created your own hilarious MAD LIBS® game!

KARATE

PERSON IN ROOM _____

ADJECTIVE_____

GEOGRAPHICAL LOCATION _____

PLURAL NOUN _____

NOUN _____

SILLY WORD_____

NOUN _____

JAPANESE WORD_____

NOUN _____

NOUN _____

ADJECTIVE_____

ADVERB_____

SILLY WORD_____

VERB _____

NOUN _____

PART OF THE BODY_____

MAD LIBS®
KARATE

Tomorrow, the famous Japanese karate master, _____,
PERSON IN ROOM

will be giving _____ lessons in the recreation hall. Karate
ADJECTIVE

was invented 700 years ago in _____ . It is a
GEOGRAPHICAL LOCATION

method of self-defense which turns your hands and feet into deadly

_____ . Other martial arts are _____ , Jujitsu,
PLURAL NOUN   NOUN

and Kung _____ . All of them will enable you to defeat any
SILLY WORD

_____ who attacks you. The hip throw, known as the
NOUN

_____ , works like this: You put your right _____
JAPANESE WORD   NOUN

behind your opponent's left _____ and pull down on his
NOUN

_____ arm. Do this _____ . As you pull,
ADJECTIVE   ADVERB

shout, "_____ !" very loudly. This should _____
SILLY WORD   VERB

your opponent's collar bone and dislocate his _____ .
NOUN

If it doesn't, try again with your other _____ .
PART OF THE BODY

From CAMP DAZE MAD LIBS® • Copyright © 2001, 1988 by Penguin Random House LLC.

MAD LIBS® is fun to play with friends, but you can also play it by yourself! To begin with, DO NOT look at the story on the page below. Fill in the blanks on this page with the words called for. Then, using the words you have selected, fill in the blank spaces in the story.

Now you've created your own hilarious MAD LIBS® game!

FOURTH OF JULY

NUMBER _____

MONTH _____

ADJECTIVE _____

NOUN _____

ADJECTIVE _____

NOUN _____

NOUN _____

ADJECTIVE _____

PLURAL NOUN _____

PLURAL NOUN _____

PLURAL NOUN _____

ADJECTIVE _____

NOUN _____

NOUN _____

NOUN _____

PLURAL NOUN _____

PLURAL NOUN _____

PLURAL NOUN _____

ADJECTIVE _____

ADVERB _____

VERB _____

PLURAL NOUN _____

NOUN _____

MAD☺LIBS®
FOURTH OF JULY

Every year on the _____ th of _____ , we celebrate the Fourth
               NUMBER   MONTH

of July. This holiday commemorates the birth of our _____
                                           ADJECTIVE

_____ . Many _____ citizens observe
     NOUN   ADJECTIVE

Independence _____ by hanging their _____
                NOUN   NOUN

from a window or by running it up a/an _____ pole.
                                 ADJECTIVE

Most _____ spend this holiday at home with family and
     PLURAL NOUN

_____ or visit national _____ or _____
 PLURAL NOUN   PLURAL NOUN   ADJECTIVE

beaches. Food as American as apple _____ , hamburgers,
                               NOUN

and corn on the _____ are traditional holiday _____ .
               NOUN   NOUN

And in the evening, there are displays of _____ , such
                                 PLURAL NOUN

as Roman _____ , shooting _____ , and
           PLURAL NOUN   PLURAL NOUN

_____ rockets which _____ _____
 ADJECTIVE   ADVERB   VERB

the sky. A word of caution: Do not use _____ unless
                                 PLURAL NOUN

you are supervised by a knowledgeable _____ .
                                 NOUN

MAD LIBS® is fun to play with friends, but you can also play it by yourself! To begin with, DO NOT look at the story on the page below. Fill in the blanks on this page with the words called for. Then, using the words you have selected, fill in the blank spaces in the story.

Now you've created your own hilarious MAD LIBS® game!

SWIMMING

VERB ENDING IN "ING" _____

VERB ENDING IN "ING" _____

PLURAL NOUN _____

VERB _____

PLURAL NOUN _____

NOUN _____

PLURAL NOUN _____

ANIMAL _____

NATIONALITY _____

NOUN _____

ADJECTIVE _____

COLOR _____

ADJECTIVE _____

PERSON IN ROOM _____

MAD☺LIBS®
SWIMMING

Swimming is easier than _____ or _____.
                        VERB ENDING IN "ING"   VERB ENDING IN "ING"

There are more Americans who swim than there are _____
                                                      PLURAL NOUN

who _____. This is because many Americans have
          VERB

swimming _____. It's not hard to swim. First you learn
              PLURAL NOUN

to float on your _____. Then you practice kicking your
                      NOUN

_____ until you do the _____-paddle. Then you
     PLURAL NOUN   ANIMAL

can go on to the _____ crawl. Later you can master the
                      NATIONALITY

_____ stroke and the _____ stroke. If you learn
        NOUN   ADJECTIVE

all of these, someday you may get into the Olympics and win a/an

_____ medal and get to do TV commercials for _____
        COLOR   ADJECTIVE

companies and become as famous as _____.
                                        PERSON IN ROOM

MAD LIBS® is fun to play with friends, but you can also play it by yourself! To begin with, DO NOT look at the story on the page below. Fill in the blanks on this page with the words called for. Then, using the words you have selected, fill in the blank spaces in the story.

Now you've created your own hilarious MAD LIBS® game!

SCUBA DIVING

PLURAL NOUN _____

FIVE LETTERS OF THE ALPHABET _____

PLURAL NOUN STARTING WITH "A" _____

TYPE OF GAS _____

PART OF THE BODY (PLURAL) _____

TYPE OF LIQUID _____

ADJECTIVE_____

VERB _____

TYPE OF FISH (PLURAL)_____

PLURAL NOUN _____

PLURAL NOUN _____

TYPE OF REPTILE_____

TYPE OF VEHICLE (PLURAL)_____

PLURAL NOUN _____

PLURAL NOUN _____

MAD LIBS®
SCUBA DIVING

There are camps which teach their _____ how to scuba dive.
PLURAL NOUN

The word "scuba," which is spelled _____, means
FIVE LETTERS OF THE ALPHABET

"self-contained underwater breathing _____."
PLURAL NOUN STARTING WITH "A"

Scuba divers wear a tank filled with _____ strapped on their
TYPE OF GAS

backs and a mask over their _____. They can stay
PART OF THE BODY (PLURAL)

submerged in _____ for as long as two hours. Scuba divers
TYPE OF LIQUID

must be in _____ physical condition to _____
ADJECTIVE   VERB

underwater. They're liable to run into man-eating _____
TYPE OF FISH (PLURAL)

or poisonous _____. Scuba divers have discovered
PLURAL NOUN

many sunken _____. In the U.S. Navy, they are called
PLURAL NOUN

_____-men. And in World War II, they sank many enemy
TYPE OF REPTILE

_____ by swimming underneath them and fastening
TYPE OF VEHICLE (PLURAL)

_____ to their _____.
PLURAL NOUN   PLURAL NOUN

MAD LIBS® is fun to play with friends, but you can also play it by yourself! To begin with, DO NOT look at the story on the page below. Fill in the blanks on this page with the words called for. Then, using the words you have selected, fill in the blank spaces in the story.

Now you've created your own hilarious MAD LIBS® game!

LETTER OF RECOMMENDATION

RELATIVE _____

PERSON IN ROOM (MALE)_____

NOUN _____

ADJECTIVE_____

SCHOOL _____

VERB ENDING IN "ING" _____

PLURAL NOUN _____

TYPE OF GAME _____

ADJECTIVE_____

PLURAL NOUN _____

SAME NOUN, SINGULAR_____

ADJECTIVE_____

ADJECTIVE_____

ANIMAL _____

ANIMAL _____

NOUN _____

ADJECTIVE_____

NOUN _____

ADJECTIVE_____

NOUN _____

Dear Director:

I would like to recommend my _____ , _____ ,
RELATIVE   PERSON IN ROOM (MALE)

for the job of assistant _____ in your _____
NOUN   ADJECTIVE

camp. He has just graduated from _____ and has a
SCHOOL

degree in _____ . He has had experience teaching
VERB ENDING IN "ING"

_____ how to play _____ . He is ambitious
PLURAL NOUN   TYPE OF GAME

and _____ . During school vacations, he used to work
ADJECTIVE

delivering for _____ , our neighborhood _____
PLURAL NOUN   SAME NOUN (SINGULAR)

store. He is a loyal and _____ person and will make a
ADJECTIVE

very _____ counselor because he will work like a/an
ADJECTIVE

_____ and he is as smart as a/an _____ . He
ANIMAL   ANIMAL

is also as honest as the _____ is long. I promise you
NOUN

that this _____ _____ will make a very
ADJECTIVE   NOUN

_____ counselor for your _____ .
ADJECTIVE   NOUN

MAD LIBS® is fun to play with friends, but you can also play it by yourself! To begin with, DO NOT look at the story on the page below. Fill in the blanks on this page with the words called for. Then, using the words you have selected, fill in the blank spaces in the story.

Now you've created your own hilarious MAD LIBS® game!

CANOEING

FOREIGN WORD _____

NUMBER _____

ADJECTIVE _____

ADJECTIVE _____

NOUN _____

PLURAL NOUN _____

ADJECTIVE _____

NOUN _____

TYPE OF LIQUID _____

VERB _____

NOUN _____

PLURAL NOUN _____

NOUN _____

NOUN _____

VERB (PAST TENSE) _____

VERB ENDING IN "ING" _____

ADJECTIVE _____

NOUN _____

MAD☺LIBS®
CANOEING

"Canoe" comes from the Spanish word "_____." This

FOREIGN WORD

type of vessel was first described by Columbus in the year _____.

NUMBER

It is a/an _____ boat with its sides meeting in a/an

ADJECTIVE

_____ edge at each _____. A canoe is moved by

ADJECTIVE · NOUN

one or more _____. It is important for you to learn the

PLURAL NOUN

_____ way to paddle your _____ before putting

ADJECTIVE · NOUN

it in the _____. Should your canoe overturn and you do

TYPE OF LIQUID

not know how to _____, hang onto the side of the

VERB

_____, kick your _____, and head for the

NOUN · PLURAL NOUN

safety of the _____. If you surface under the canoe,

NOUN

locate the air _____, which will allow you to breathe until

NOUN

you are _____. Once you have mastered the art of

VERB (PAST TENSE)

_____, you can enjoy an overnight _____

VERB ENDING IN "ING" · ADJECTIVE

trip, which often is the highlight of the camping _____.

NOUN

MAD LIBS® is fun to play with friends, but you can also play it by yourself! To begin with, DO NOT look at the story on the page below. Fill in the blanks on this page with the words called for. Then, using the words you have selected, fill in the blank spaces in the story.

Now you've created your own hilarious MAD LIBS® game!

PLANTS

PLURAL NOUN _____

COLOR_____

PLURAL NOUN _____

COLOR_____

ADJECTIVE_____

PLURAL NOUN _____

TYPE OF LIQUID _____

NOUN _____

PLURAL NOUN _____

NOUN _____

VERB _____

ANOTHER TYPE OF LIQUID _____

NOUN _____

PLURAL NOUN _____

NOUN _____

ADJECTIVE_____

ANIMAL (PLURAL) _____

PLURAL NOUN _____

MAD LIBS®
PLANTS

How to recognize the flora and _____ around your campsite.
  PLURAL NOUN

1. A pine tree is very tall and _____. Instead of leaves,
   COLOR

   it has millions of tiny little _____.
   PLURAL NOUN

2. A cypress is shorter and is more of a/an _____. Cypresses
   COLOR

   can be used for Christmas trees if they are not too _____.
   ADJECTIVE

3. A poison ivy bush has copper-colored _____. It
   PLURAL NOUN

   secretes a pungent _____, and if it gets on your hands
   TYPE OF LIQUID

   or _____, it will cause you to break out in red
   NOUN

   _____ and itch.
   PLURAL NOUN

4. A skunk is a cute little rodent with a big, bushy black and white

   _____. If you _____ it or frighten it, it will
   NOUN   **VERB**

   squirt you with skunk _____, and for a week you
   ANOTHER TYPE OF LIQUID

   will smell like a rotten _____.
   NOUN

5. Mulberries are very sweet little _____ that grow
   PLURAL NOUN

   on a big tree. Be careful not to eat too many or you will get a/an

   _____ ache.
   NOUN

6. Walnuts often grow wild. They are a very _____ nut, and you
   ADJECTIVE

   can eat them. Walnuts are the favorite food of _____,
   ANIMAL (PLURAL)

   who store them in hollow _____.
   PLURAL NOUN

From CAMP DAZE MAD LIBS® • Copyright © 2001, 1988 by Penguin Random House LLC.

MAD LIBS® is fun to play with friends, but you can also play it by yourself! To begin with, DO NOT look at the story on the page below. Fill in the blanks on this page with the words called for. Then, using the words you have selected, fill in the blank spaces in the story.

Now you've created your own hilarious MAD LIBS® game!

HIKING

ADJECTIVE _____

NOUN _____

VERB ENDING IN "ING" _____

ADJECTIVE _____

PLURAL NOUN _____

PART OF THE BODY (PLURAL) _____

DIRECTION _____

ANIMAL (PLURAL) _____

NOUN _____

PLURAL NOUN _____

VERB ENDING IN "ING" _____

ADJECTIVE _____

NUMBER _____

NOUN _____

ADJECTIVE _____

ADVERB _____

HIKING

Hiking is a really _____ thing to do in the summer.
ADJECTIVE

But, hiking is nothing like going for a walk in the _____ or
NOUN

_____ around the house. The serious hiker needs lots
VERB ENDING IN "ING"

of _____ equipment. You must have very comfortable
ADJECTIVE

_____ so you won't make your _____ sore.
PLURAL NOUN   PART OF THE BODY (PLURAL)

If you hike in a forest, you must take a compass so you can tell which

direction is _____ , and you must carry bits of food so you
DIRECTION

can feed the _____ . Every good hiker wears a
ANIMAL (PLURAL)

backpack, which contains a rolled-up_____ and some extra
NOUN

_____ . If you plan to stay overnight, you must have a
PLURAL NOUN

fleece-lined _____ bag. Of course, if you are going up
VERB ENDING IN "ING"

a mountain, you will need even more _____ equipment.
ADJECTIVE

You will need a/an _____-foot rope and metal pistons to pound
NUMBER

into the side of whatever _____ you are scaling.
NOUN

Remember all these _____ tips and you will be able to
ADJECTIVE

get back home _____ .
ADVERB

MAD LIBS® is fun to play with friends, but you can also play it by yourself! To begin with, DO NOT look at the story on the page below. Fill in the blanks on this page with the words called for. Then, using the words you have selected, fill in the blank spaces in the story.

Now you've created your own hilarious MAD LIBS® game!

EXPLORERS

PERSON IN ROOM _____

CELEBRITY _____

SPANISH WORD_____

PLURAL NOUN _____

SAME SPANISH WORD _____

ADJECTIVE_____

SOMETHING WET _____

PLACE _____

NUMBER _____

ADJECTIVE_____

TYPE OF LIQUID _____

ADJECTIVE_____

ADJECTIVE_____

VERB ENDING IN "ING" _____

PLURAL NOUN _____

NOUN _____

ADJECTIVE_____

SOMETHING ALIVE (PLURAL) _____

Camping is a good way to learn to be an explorer. Famous explorers have been Columbus, Pizarro, Balboa, and _____,
PERSON IN ROOM
who discovered _____. Hernando Cortes was a Spanish
CELEBRITY
_____ who came to South America and conquered
SPANISH WORD
the _____. Francisco Pizarro was another famous
PLURAL NOUN
_____. He was the first man to see the _____
SAME SPANISH WORD   ADJECTIVE
Pacific _____. Ponce de Leon discovered Puerto
SOMETHING WET
Rico, Florida, and _____ in 1512. He spent _____
PLACE   NUMBER
years in Florida trying to find a/an _____ fountain of youth.
ADJECTIVE
He believed that _____ from this fountain would make him
TYPE OF LIQUID
eternally _____. He marched his _____ troops
ADJECTIVE   ADJECTIVE
through swamps _____ with alligators and
VERB ENDING IN "ING"
_____ in search of this miracle _____ but
PLURAL NOUN   NOUN
never found anything that would make him _____. The
ADJECTIVE
only thing he found were thousands of _____
SOMETHING ALIVE (PLURAL)
from the north who had come there for a vacation.

MAD LIBS® is fun to play with friends, but you can also play it by yourself! To begin with, DO NOT look at the story on the page below. Fill in the blanks on this page with the words called for. Then, using the words you have selected, fill in the blank spaces in the story.

Now you've created your own hilarious MAD LIBS® game!

CAMP SONGS

ADJECTIVE _____

NOUN _____

PLURAL NOUN _____

ADJECTIVE _____

SOMETHING ALIVE _____

ADJECTIVE _____

ADJECTIVE _____

NOUN _____

NOUN _____

ADJECTIVE _____

NOUN _____

ADJECTIVE _____

VERB ENDING IN "ING" _____

PLURAL NOUN _____

VERB ENDING IN "ING" _____

NOUN _____

NOUN _____

CAMP SONGS

A/an _____ activity at camp is to gather around the
　　　　　ADJECTIVE

_____ in the evening and roast _____
　　　NOUN　　　　　　　　　　　　　　　　　　　　　　　　PLURAL NOUN

while singing _____ songs accompanied by a/an
　　　　　　　　　　ADJECTIVE

_____ on the harmonica. A/an _____
SOMETHING ALIVE　　　　　　　　　　　　　　　　　　　　ADJECTIVE

survey tells us the most popular _____ songs are
　　　　　　　　　　　　　　　　　　ADJECTIVE

"Row, Row, Row Your _____," "She'll Be Coming Around
　　　　　　　　　　　NOUN

the _____," "By the Light of the _____
　　　NOUN　　　　　　　　　　　　　　　　　　　　　　　ADJECTIVE

_____," "Down By the _____ Mill Stream,"
　　NOUN　　　　　　　　　　　　　　　ADJECTIVE

"I've Been _____ on the Railroad," "When the
　　　　　VERB ENDING IN "ING"

_____ Go _____ In," "Swing Low Sweet
PLURAL NOUN　　　　　　VERB ENDING IN "ING"

_____," and "Home, Home on the _____."
　　NOUN　　　　　　　　　　　　　　　　　　　　　　　NOUN

Download Mad Libs today!

Join the millions of Mad Libs fans creating wacky and wonderful stories on our apps!